Forgiveness Generates Internal Vital Energy

Patricia L. McDonald

DORRANCE PUBLISHING CO., INC.
PITTSBURGH, PENNSYLVANIA 15222

ISBN # 0-8059-4685-3
Printed in the United States of America

Second Printing

For information or to order additional books, please write:
Dorrance Publishing Co., Inc.
643 Smithfield Street
Pittsburgh, Pennsylvania 15222
U.S.A.
1-800-788-7654

Contents

FOREWORD

My life journey has taken me to many parts of the United States and countries abroad, the latest being France and the Ukraine. Through my journeys, readings, and conversations with the many people I have met, I have come to the conclusion that along with other needs such as compassion and love, there is the need of forgiveness. Yet, if we allow pride and stubbornness to enter, take rest, and become rooted, then our life journey, our spirit journey, our energetic ability, and our creative potential to live life to the fullest suffer tremendously.

When we do not forgive, all relationships are fractured. We impair relationships with self, other people, the many systems in which we operate on a continual basis, and even with God. We are not whole nor can we be. Even our immune system is affected by negative emotions, often without conscious awareness. Our immune system continually eavesdrops on our thoughts. Our bodies are a physical manifestation of that which we carry within. We are the sum total of all our thoughts.

As we reflect on the content of these pages, the focus will be to view forgiveness from a personal and professional viewpoint. A personal viewpoint toward forgiveness could center on relationships within our family structure. It could also encompass persons to whom we relate at work, school, our neighborhoods, or our social groups. Persons who possess some semblance of control over us, or we over them, could be unconsciously affected by a lack of forgiveness.

A professional focus involving forgiveness could involve others who have power, influence, and authority over us. It could also include co-workers. It could include people with whom we have some type of professional connection on either a formal or an informal basis.

At times we need to see it from both viewpoints, and at other times we need to place our energy more in one area than in another. It is important to note, though, that one viewpoint affects the other. Both personal and professional forgiveness can generate internal vital energy.

Forgiveness, the word, will be seen often throughout the pages of this book. I will offer insight and awareness into analyzing a definition of forgiveness along with an interpretation. When the components of forgiveness are understood, the power they possess can be internalized. We can then process and analyze the various aspects of our existence. By looking at forgiveness, or the lack of it, we can come to understand its awesome significance in our lives.

I have had the privilege of having participants in my workshops reveal personal stories, situations, events, or happenings that occurred, sometimes recently but often many years ago. Some indicate they hold onto situations, events, or memory and, thus, are inhibited from moving toward a desired direction in a positive fashion. They just cannot let go of the action, deed, event, situation, or word. The pain and suffering at times are critically limiting. The difficult task of forgiving others for their words or actions is real and keeps "forward movement" in check.

It is my hope that the words, thoughts, or questions the reader finds on these pages will heal some wounds. The reader, when healed, can move on to a deeper level of living with fuller energy, thus enhancing personal spirituality and living life in a charged fashion.

Forgiveness, when fully understood and realized, can indeed generate internal vital energy. Energy that we need for placing our body, mind, heart, and soul into living in the here and now can be ours while working toward a healthier and holier future.

My appreciation to:

Sean Therese Halpin and **Florence Gibbons** for their early proof-reading.

Sharon O'Brien for her editing expertise.

Melissa Sissen, Siena Heights University, Public Relations Librarian, for her general publishing experience

Those **individuals named** throughout this manuscript who have shared their personal stories concerning forgiveness.

My **Adrian Dominican** connections.

Two significant friends who have taught me profound truths and have helped me grow in ways beyond measure, **Marge Naber** and **Peg O'Flynn.**

My **family,** to whom I dedicate this book.

Family Tree

JOSEPH ALOYSIUS MC DONALD 3-15-1897 (d. 10-12-73) &
ETHEL IRENE REYNOLDS 6-10-1906 (d.7-9-74)

CATHERINE 11-16-27 (d. 2-13-98) & Ralph Clark 12-23-20
    Andrea   4-24-50 & Larry Russell 10-23-50
                   =Aimee 6-8-73, Geoffrey 5-24-75, Casey 9-20-76
    Don   7-5-51 & Darlene 9-1-56
                   =Stacy Lynn, 8-26-79, Kristi 10-28-81
    Keith   6-30-61 & Krista 10-29-52

JOSEPH   9-16-29 & Dolores Girrback 1-5-27 (d.2-2-95)
    Michael   10-10-52 & Cathy Mooney 9-24-57
                   =Theresa Mooney 11-8-81, Elizabeth Mooney 8-9-83
                   =Kathy Mooney 10-11-85
                   =Lauren McDonald 3-20-95, Jenny McDonald 7-25-96
    Chris   12-25-53 & Diane 4-11-53
                   =James 10-22-87, Anthony 11-3-88
    Patrick   7-10-58 & Ann Millsap 4-9-58
                   =Matthew Moss 11-26-80, Sarah Grace 2-8-88,
                   Patrick Joseph II 10-1-91, Jacob Xavier 11-12-97
    Colleen   7-2-59 & Terry Laurain 1-5-50
                   =Therese 12-20-83, Daniel 12-13-85, Terry Laurain, Jr. 4-11-95

MARJORIE 1-21-31 & Robert Crocker 8-4-22

ROBERT 10-29-34 (d. 12-13-87) & Kay Slark 8-6-36
    Michael   4-6-58 & Mary
                   =Fabien 11-3-84, Andrew 2-25-86
    Leigh   8-24-62
SALLY 8-11-36 & Rudy Morales Sr. 11-10-35
    Rudy Jr.   4-2-55 & Joyce Jennings 11-26-54
                   =Andrew Jennings 10-21-78, Nicole 6-6-83
    Colleen   5-2-58 & Frank DiMattia 7-14-54
                   =Elizabeth 6-6-77, Robert 5-2-79
    Ralph   1-22-66 & Gabriella 10-3-66
                   =Victoria Dee 8-29-91, Adalina 10-6-93, Ralphael Jose Jr. 7-28-98

RUTH 2-16-38 & Josa Sosa 11-10-24 (d. 3-13-83)
    Harold   10-29-59 & Laura & Antonia 3-29-96
                   =James & Joseph 2-11-78, Jonathon 8-1-87, Joshua 5-26-93
                   =Kathleen Anita 10-4-91
                   =Sergie 6-17-82
    Bettye   10-21-60 & Anthony Lukasiewicz 5-27-58
                   =Eric 4-27-87, Ellen Marie 4-12-90, Kathleen 8-29-92
    Leslie   8-17-67 & Javier Cuellar 5-23-59
                   =Jason 10-10-89, Brittini 10-9-90, Manuel 5-14-94,
                   Daniel Jose 10-5-98
    Felisa   9-5-68 & Ron Wambold
                   =Marcus & Michael 9-23-89
    Matthew 10-11-78

JAMES 9-15-40

LOUISE   10-9-41 & Anthony Morabto 8-23-25
    Jennie   7-27-62 & Ervin Reed 6-17-71
                   =Taylor Louise 10-4-98

MARY 6-10-43 & Donald Steele 10-25-40
    Tami   4-29-68 & Brian Clayton 6-17-66
    Krista   3-5-71

PAT 4-5-45

Chapter I

FORGIVENESS: DEFINITIONS

FOR <u>GIVE</u> NESS
<u>G</u>enerates
<u>I</u>nternal
<u>V</u>ital
<u>E</u>nergy

Personally, Professionally, and Spiritually

Could my life be different with a new awareness of forgiveness? Am I maximizing my potential in all areas of my existence, primarily in the personal areas, which include family, friends, and associates? Is my professional focus, which includes colleagues at work and business associates, moving in the directions I have intended? Or is the spiritual direction of my energy leading me down avenues toward life?

What does forgiveness mean? Why would I need to think differently? What is available to me in the explorations of new insights surrounding forgiveness? My mental patterns of thought and personal issues of behavior have served me this far in life, so why do they need to be changed? Why devote new energy toward this topic?

In the exploration of any subject, it is always best to begin with a definition, a common understanding which is universally acceptable. An understanding provides a base and measure of comparison. Let us first explore a familiar resource that has been around for decades.

Webster's Dictionary (1990, p. 233) states that to forgive means:

1. to give up resentment against or the desire to punish;
2. stop being angry with; pardon
3. to give up all claim to punish or to exact penalty for (an offense); to overlook
4. to cancel or remit (a debt).

Another view of forgiveness is offered by Caroline Myss, who states in *Anatomy of the Spirit* (1996, p. 215), "Forgiveness is a complex act of consciousness, one that liberates the psyche and soul from the need for personal vengeance and the perception of oneself as a victim."

Many adults carry situations, events, memories well beyond the "life years" of the events. Often we hear of people concentrating on memories that are so old that only the carrier remembers any of the circumstances (often the perpetrator is many years dead). Bass and Davis (1988, p. 149) remember one individual's recollection: "I'll never forgive my father. It would be a lot different if he had come to me at any point in time and said, 'I'm sorry for what I've done. I've hurt you terribly. I'm going to get myself in therapy. I'm going to work this out.' But he's never done anything like that."

Such a response indicates that the one who has been hurt is still focusing on self rather than coming to an understanding, condition, or insight as to what may have caused the action so long ago.

Bass and Davis (1988, p.1) provide unique insight into forgiveness, its meaning, and its actions. They state:

To find out exactly what forgiveness is, we looked in the dictionary and found these definitions:

a). to cease to feel resentment against an offender;

b). to give up claim to requital from an offender;

c). to grant relief from payment

There are, then, two elements in what we call forgiveness. One is that you give up your anger and no longer blame the abuser, you excuse him/her for what was done to you. The other element is that you no longer try to get some kind of compensation from the abuser. You give up trying to get financial compensation, a statement of guilt, an apology, respect, love, understanding—anything. Separating these two aspects of forgiveness makes it possible to clarify what is and what is not necessary in order to heal.

Of all the great teachers we study, from past to present, and all the organized teaching from the world religions, Jesus, with His message of love, was the first and only one to stress "forgiveness." The great teachers of life, those who have made a place in history, as well as those who have made a place in our hearts, continually emphasize the value of "letting go."

In addition to the dictionary and current authors as indicated, we can always resort to Jesus' command to "forgive seventy times seven." He also taught us to love one another as He loved us. If we are to take these words to heart, and forgive offenses, then appropriate responses need to follow. Listening to new applications of forgiveness can be the genesis of renewed life.

As we think about the content of this message, our focus will be to view forgiveness from both a personal as well as a professional point of view. At times we need to do both, and at other times we need to place our focus and energy more in one area than the other. It is important to note, though, that one effects the other. Personal forgiveness generates energy which carries into our professional lives. In addition we benefit within our spiritual realm of living life with full energy, with a spirited focus and toward a renewed purpose.

We look at this symbol of energy. It is clear that action begets action. It serves to keep life in motion personally, professionally, and spiritually.

Check out the movement of your life.

"Unforgiving action" limits potential in numerous arenas of our lives. Holding onto "heavies" restricts personal growth and development, whether or not we are conscious of it. By not letting go, we use energy to merely "hang on," that could be used elsewhere. The longer we continue stuffing old wounds, the more we diminish our current state, and future potential, and the more we hurt ourselves.

3

HOW MUCH DO YOU HURT — "OUTSIDE?"

Now isn't that a strange question? Well yes and no! It's strange because we generally only ask it in regard to a physical hurt or injury. We understand what physical pain does to our mind, heart, and body. It limits our potential in all aspects of life. We experience curtailment of forward movement. We are halted in furthering our progress. In experiencing physical pain, we want to take direction, heal what is injured, and get back to doing what we intended to do. A physical injury gets a lot of attention.

We look at the "movement" these pictures
symbolize and say go, go, go!

Just watch a sports event on television and you will soon see how much attention is given to an injured athlete, especially the star player. The public does not want its star out of action. Subsequently a great deal of media attention is focused on that person. The trainers and coaches are encouraged to deliver whatever assistance is needed, sparing no expense, to get him back onto the field to perform. After all this is how the individual will earn a living, so a great deal of focus is getting back to the "maximum" performance level.

Ah! This we understand. This body does have to heal to perform physically. We want it that way. We do all we can to achieve this goal. Even if one needs some physical adaptive equipment to get on track, then it is provided in urgent quantity and quality.

To get back in motion is the goal.

Now that this concept of our physical importance is clear and easy to comprehend, let's move on to another area of life. What do we do when we ask the same question, "How much do you hurt," yet the injury is not visible, but on the inside. It cannot be seen. Others do not have insight, awareness, or knowledge of the pain we carry within. Many times people choose not to disclose their painful past. A choice is made to try and move through life with buried episodes from the past. We keep injuries to ourselves and try to work around them. Where do we get the power to identify inner pain and access the necessary resources to deal with a situation? Do we even know assistance can be accessed? No individual has to live in a negative, dark, unforgiving past!

HOW MUCH DO YOU HURT INSIDE?
The question of inside hurt is perplexing. Often it cannot be readily named. Hurt on the inside can be emotional, physical, psychological, sexual, or spiritual, and is not easily responded to in most conversations. Often the reality of "inside hurt" is denied for fear of upsetting a current mode of operation. Routines are not to be disturbed. Bringing up unpleasentries disturbs equilibrium. Why draw attention to something which is primarily internal? We have not been programmed to address inner hurt and pain. For a long time, society required that we deny their very existence.

As internal hurt and pain are explored, we know they connect to and affect our heart, mind, body, and soul. All of life is interwoven, every part of the universe is connected. The visuals below help us see that when we hurt on the inside, all aspects of life and relationships are affected.

5

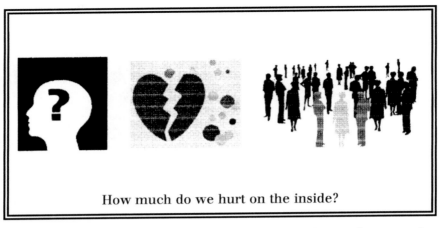

How much do we hurt on the inside?

The response to the question how much do we hurt on the inside now takes on an entirely new focus. This can prove to be challenging. What are we willing to disclose about the answer(s) to that question? Can we even admit the hurt? How do we even begin to comprehend the limitations of our mind, heart, and body when we cannot even identify the location of our hurt?

Is our inside hurt so multifaceted that we don't know where to begin? Possibly we don't even recognize our inside hurt. How, then, can we identify it, as well as its impact on our life? We begin to question ourselves and say, "Where do I even begin to address the issue? How do I start?"

Too often we cannot identify the location of our hurt because it is so deeply imbedded in our psyche. We squelch the events so we can get through our days. Over time we establish ways to cope. Previous pain is sometimes difficult to locate because it is:

1. suppressed
2. compressed
3. depressed
4. ignored
5. complex
6. interconnected
7. multifaceted
8. hidden
9. not discernible to the naked eye
10. etc.,

Situations affect our ability to maximize the potential that could be ours.

The hurt(s) we carry inhibit our complete growth and development in nebulous ways. Frequently we are not even conscious of their residual effects. Often there is an abundance of matter we carry "inside" which effects our "outside." The internal vital energy we need just to exist goes in directions that do not bring about the good for which it is designed. The generation of internal vital energy goes into ways and means which do not effect our optimal being. Growth and development happen, but often not in a positive direction. Settel, in *The Book of Gandhi Wisdom* (1995, p. 134), states "the body which contains a diseased mind can never be anything but diseased." Thus, let us return to the two questions at the beginning of this section.

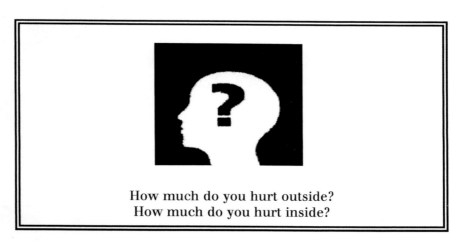

How much do you hurt outside?
How much do you hurt inside?

Let us explore a definition of "forgiveness" offered by this author: ***"forgiveness means generating internal vital energy."*** This definition of forgiveness is very personal indeed. By forgiving we allow the release of essential energetic power to sanction future potential. It has such profound connections to our total being that often we do not realize its tremendous all-encompassing power.

One way of thinking about the awesome connection of 1) mind, 2) heart, 3) body, and 4) soul is the thought that our immune system is continually eavesdropping on our thoughts. What an awareness!

We have scientific awareness of three lines of evidence of mind-body connection according to Goleman and Gurin in their *Mind/Body, Medicine* (1993, p. 8), when they offer the following insights.

The scientific evidence for the mind's influence on the body now comes from three converging areas of research:

1. *Physiological* research, which investigates the biological and biochemical connections between the brain and the body's systems.

2. *Epidemiological* research, which shows a correlation between certain psychological factors and certain illnesses in the population at large.

3. *Clinical* research, which tests the effectiveness of mind/body approaches in preventing, alleviating, or treating specific diseases.

We can do so much more when our body and mind are balanced.

FORGIVENESS: REPROGRAMMING

Forgiveness is turning toward new light. It involves the reprogramming of thought, word, action, or deed into an alternative mental reservoir. Forgiveness is that conscious act in which we place ourselves in an arena of hope, life, energy, and action. Forgiveness affords a new surge in living life fully alive!

To commit an act of forgiveness is a huge admission that previous courses were not actively beneficial. This is not so much an admission of guilt, but rather an awareness that we are not making sufficient progress in a positive life direction. When we do not actively partake in an act of forgiveness, the consequences have a ripple effect. The progress of life isn't always an optimistic journey when we carry old discarded negativity. Recipients of our lack of forgiveness can be:

- self
- parents
- siblings

- spouse
- children
- friends
- employees
- systems
- communities

We are human beings, which implies taking an active part in the direction we live, the choices we make, and the relationship we maintain with all others to whom we are connected. The list above helps us to think with clear vision about those who play a part in our growth and development. It matters if we hold unfinished business with or grudges toward anyone. We all need to reflect on our list as individuals and assess how a lack of forgiveness could have negative consequences in our day-to-day world.

We have not yet begun to realize the tremendous power that lies within the human mind. Reprogramming offers new vision. *The ability to be creative is staggering.* So much of our potential never gets tapped. Our creative space is darkened with old, dingy pictures or images. We are often too busy living in another time and space. By understanding what forgiveness does, and what it does not do, we can create a new life force.

Action and energy cause change to happen. Being "for" something, i.e., forgiving, indicates a willingness to move in a new or alternative direction. Movement can take a form or direction in an individual on various levels.

Let us spend a few moments and do some personal reflection on the diverse aspects of our lives. See how either stagnation or inhibition grow due to the connections we have with ourselves and with one another:

- emotionally   = are we flat or alive; is there emotional balance
- physically   = what attention is our body given
  - = how do we take care of this million dollar machine
- psychologically   = is our cognitive ability well stabilized
  - = do we use sound judgment on a regular basis
- sexually   = do we experience a wholeness, a completed self
  - = do I value how I was created
- spiritually   = does our spirited life reflect aliveness to others
  - = does my life generate life

As we look at the word "forgiveness," we understand that the implementation of its meaning indicates movement, movement that can occur in multiple designs or in diverse facets of our being. It is important to realize that some movement does need to occur! Each person has to look at his or her personal and professional areas of stagnation and do some inner search. What are we, and how are we, in the various pieces of our daily living and corresponding interactions? Often we experience a deterioration before our own eyes, yet we cannot see.

The seeing and recognizing are inhibited because we have not forgiven someone or some thing. It is important to note that this could be either conscious or unconscious. The mind can produce such a power surge if we get rid of the dust.

A powerful way of viewing "forgiveness" is the modification of one's views and beliefs. Change necessitates action in thought form. Many of our thoughts need modification, alteration, enhancing, downsizing, right-sizing, up-sizing, compacting, narrowing, adjusting, and, most of all, balance. Thoughts, words, actions, and deeds need reevaluation on a periodic basis. We each need reflective time, space, and a comfortable environment. It is only when we take stock of the components of our life that we can make adjustments. We can't take action when there is no evaluation.

By viewing the course of action in many arenas of life, our personal life, as well as the professional component and, most important, our spiritual life, we assess the quantity and quality of our being. Then we can look at how the balance in our life has taken form.

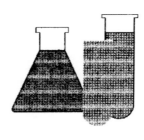

Forgiveness generates internal vital energy
and brings us balance.

Chapter II

WHY FORGIVENESS IS SO HARD

Forgiveness is hard because change is hard. Change necessitates alteration. Change means reforming, reconstructing, remodeling, rearranging, reorganizing. Note the "ing" in all these verbs. They are action words. Forgiveness necessitates personal transformation. A movement towards "new" form. Letting go of the "old." It is a movement toward removal of previous thoughts, words, actions, behavior, or patterns.

Forgiveness is difficult at times because when we forgive we are forced to move on, to take ourselves in another direction, to move into a different arena of life and living. When forgiveness does not occur, we know the consequences:

- aches
- close-mindedness
- emotional imbalance
- isolation
- mental anguish
- pain
- rigidity
- tears

But when we can forgive, we arrive at a new state of being.

Chapter III

IT'S TIME TO LET FORGIVENESS INTO OUR LIVES

Enter forgiveness! The interpretative meaning of forgiveness (the generation of internal vital energy), as offered here, presents a whole new and optimistic outlook.

Forgiveness exonerates! It emancipates. It is an absolution. Forgiveness means acquittal of previous conditions. It means to dispense the old, pardon the previous, and be prepared to welcome in the new. We need to develop an understanding of what happens when forgiveness does occur. For those who have forgiven, and then shared their stories, we come to know of the positive consequences of renewal. Forgiveness does all this and more. It affords us the following:

- capability
- direction
- energy
- exhilaration
- focus
- goals
- health
- might
- motion
- spirit
- steam
- strength
- vigor
- zip

Jesus offered us the "promised land" right here and now. He gifted us with this opportunity. A personalized invitation from Him awaits each of us. Come follow!

THE PROMISED LAND

Looking for our promised land could be a lifetime journey. Forgiveness guarantees the possibility of getting "new life" much sooner. Forgiveness provides for an early arrival.

When we forgive and experience a renewal, we initially recognize there was an imbalance in some aspect(s) of our being. In causing balance to occur, we must do minor or, at times, major alterations, adjustments, or modifications within our inner being or outer patterning. Forgiveness effects us emotionally, physically, psychologically, sexually, and spiritually. We generate new light in our life.

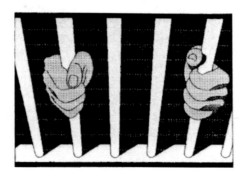

By not forgiving we keep ourselves in jail.
emotionally
physically
psychologically
sexually
spiritually

That promised land about which we dream is right here. We're standing on it. We're surrounded by it! We need look no further; rather we realize the real estate is within our midst.

Forgiveness can also be viewed as a catharsis. It is an outpouring. A catharsis is discharging socially unacceptable emotions in a socially acceptable way. Forgiveness helps us do things in the right way. If we recognize this as healthy, we can know what forgiveness can do for our heart. If *forgiveness can generate internal vital energy*, then we have to wonder what greatness can be accomplished in the multiple dimensions of our lives.

Only *you* know best what is happening. With an act of forgiveness, new energy comes into being. The old hardened ways dissipate. Previous sources of negative energy are focused into productivity, and one is hooked into a futuristic journey, into a life toward that promised land.

Forgiveness takes us in directions not previously known. It serves as a catalyst to move us into the previously uncharted territory of our own personal venue. Assessing self for untapped potential leads us to realize unmet, uncharted, unresolved capabilities. That is what forgiveness does. It leads us into places, spaces, arenas that before we could not have dreamed were attainable. Perhaps we were even unaware of their existence! The only way to find these places is to examine the courses of our lives.

Once again Settel in *The Book Of Gandhi Wisdom* (1995, p. 115) reflects "the outward freedom that we shall attain will only be in exact proportion to the inward freedom to which we may have grown at a given moment. And if this is the corrected view of freedom, our chief energy must be concentrated upon achieving reform from within."

Chapter IV

PERSONAL EVALUATION

Look at your life. Then think of all the people (frozen in time) you have met who have unknowingly been self-limiting. You have insight and awareness that their movement is minimal and, at times, nonexistent. There are many examples of self-limiting behavior to which we are continually exposed. Often we are unaware of the relationships, connections, and interweaving of our mind, body, heart, and soul. The human body is a unit of one. All aspects are related.

To help us gain insight into ourselves and others, we look at manifestations of "self-limiting" behavior. We understand this behavior as:

- hanging onto something from the past
- angry about a long-ago event
- angry toward someone who did us wrong
- fearful of taking new direction
- angry about the family system in which we grew up
- angry about what our parent(s) did or didn't do
- emotionally "flat"
- angry at self for choices made/unmade
- worried about events taking a wrong turn
- looking at situations or events in which there was involvement

The list is endless. What then can we do for a positive change?

Full awareness of what we do to ourselves is still unclear. We are unclear about the complete picture of all that can be if we are to "forgive." Forgiveness first begins with *self*. A-Ha! An important adage that we were taught so many years ago! Just how important the *self* is in all facets of life and living. Delving into *self* and what we have created for ourselves opens up options for change. The self is where it all begins. The identity of character shines though in word, in action, and, ultimately, in deed.

The management and orchestration of "self" is a really big job. In order to reassess our potential we have to take stock of what we have done up to now. Let's reflect for a few moments. Let's look at *self*, really separating the components of our being in mind, body, heart, and soul. Then we can have knowledge about how we are doing.

See how you look. Try to separate and view your 1) mind, 2) body, 3) heart, and 4) soul. To be quite honest, we cannot separate them into parts because they are all connected. However, we can look at the results of each isolated, distinguished part as related to the whole.

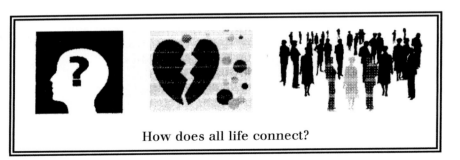

How does all life connect?

MIND
Have you ever checked into your mind's health?
What type of mental nourishment does it receive?
What is allowed entrance into your thoughts?
How old is the data that it continually absorbs?
How nutritious are the materials you take into your mind?

HEART
How is its health?
What type of care does it receive?
Can it continue to perform for you in its present state?
Is it treated with respect?
How do you respond to it on a daily basis?

BODY
How is it cared for by you?
What does it look like to you, to others?
What do you feed it on a regular basis?
How do you care for this million dollar machine?
How do you treat it?

SOUL
What nourishment does it get?
Do you give it the sacred time it needs.
How gentle are you with it?
Is it treated to the sacred space so vital to growth?
Does it receive the sacred treatment it deserves?

Forgiveness demands that we take stock of our whole person. It involves reflecting on all aspects of how we function. We are not segmented parts; we are each one entity. How then does all this fit together? As we take stock of our personal existence we ask these questions about our oneness in mind, heart, body, and soul.

How am I?
What kind of message do I convey?
As others look at me, what do they see?

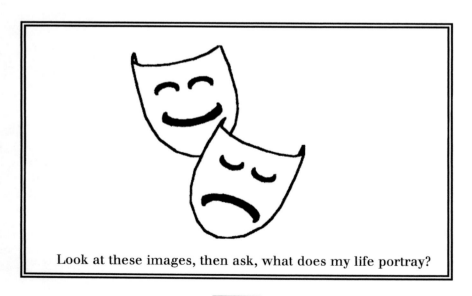

Look at these images, then ask, what does my life portray?

Chapter V

FORGIVENESS GENERATES INTERNAL VITAL ENERGY

That sentence alone places the responsibility for care of self on the individual. The body's energy is both limited and unlimited. When some of our "energy" is given over to people, areas, situations, conditions, events, and happenings in which we have no control or cannot modify, we "spend" needed energy and get "no return" on our investment. You will often hear someone make such statements as:

"I can never forgive him or her."
"The pain is just too great!"
"I'll never go back to that place again."
"Just wait, I'll get even."
"Just even thinking about the situation makes me ill."
"I'll get even if it takes me a lifetime."
"You can't image what was done to me."
"You've never been in my shoes."
"They make me so angry every time I think of them."
"They make me sick!" (they really do)

Each of us needs to take stock of what we say and do. We really do need to control the direction and subsequent outcome of our being. We need to look at what we let into our mind—thoughts, words, actions and deeds. They all matter. Every entry plays a vital part in our growth and development or our corresponding unhealthy stagnation and stuntedness. All of our parts are connected.

The internal vital energy that is within each person is used up in areas, places, and on people who, many times, have no essential connection to us on a daily basis. That's why it's important to make an assessment of where, and in whom, we are placing our very vital energy that is so sacred to our well being.

The internal aspect of forgiveness is so important to our growth and development. If we continue to harbor, nourish, and fester "old stuff," then we limit our potential for all that can be today, right now, and for our future.

In thinking about the meaning of the word forgiveness, I will offer insight and awareness for analyzing its meaning in a more detailed fashion. When the elements of forgiveness are understood, then their meaning can be weighed. We process and analyze the various aspects of our existence in all areas. By looking at forgiveness, or the lack of it, we come to understand its awesome significance in our lives. We come to gain crucial self knowledge, along with the "why" of our actions.

Let us look at the **give** in word for**give**ness and separate it into its parts. As has been said, forgiveness generates internal vital energy. Now let's take a closer look at a further dissection.

In a broad sense we could internalize forgiveness as *generating internal vital energy*.

FOR **G I V E** NESS

GENERATES:
beget
to induce
to produce
to engender
to bring into being

VITAL:
spirited
full of life
energetic
indispensable
essential to life
of crucial importance

INTERNAL:
inside
interior
intimate or secret
located further within

ENERGY:
zip
steam
potency
inherent power
capacity for action

19

By assessment of the vital aspects of this word "forgiveness," we know what needs to occur to have forgiveness happen. If we are to generate internal vital energy then we must put our emotional, physical, psychological, sexual, and spiritual forces in front of us. Forgiveness is, first of all, an internal process, after which we then externalize through action, word, or deed. We need to examine what it is that gets most of our energetic juices. Once we examine and have vision, then we must take action.

So often when the subject of forgiveness enters into a conversation, we experience a barrage of unpleasantness from an individual with negative memories. Numerous details are given about the act or actions that gave root to the aggravation. What results is a concentration of anger, frustration, hurt, and vengeance that takes over our developmental process.

It appears that all the reported action is the result of what that "other" person, group, place, system, did.

Seldom do we hear another side of the situation.

> "I may have unknowingly contributed to some
> of the resulting action."
> "What part am I responsible for in this matter?"
> "This is what I did in the process."
> "I should reflect on my actions."
> "It is time I atone for my part."
> "I was wrong."

Perhaps I need to reflect on my own attitudes and actions surrounding such behaviors affecting ageism, racism, sexism, and many of the other "ism's" plaguing humanity. It is most uncommon that one commits himself/herself to any part of the responsibility process.

This is in no way meant to infer that both sides are equally at fault, that both parties are equally to blame, or that an equality is always involved. Certainly we know that there is evil and/or total innocence in some behavior, action, or event. There are systems established, and maintained, which deny others their rightful participation. We need to view systems long and hard for what they are. Hence, we have a clearer understanding of ageism, racism, sexism, and the other "ism's" we are subjected to on a regular basis.

FORGIVENESS: A PROCESS

Forgiveness is not an easy one-time attempt, "fix-it-up" event. As Simon & Simon indicate in their work, *Forgiveness* (1990, p. 17), "Forgiveness is not a clear-cut, one-time decision."

In the journey of forgiving, we could be looking at an hour, a day, a month, perhaps a year, or maybe even most of a lifetime. Forgiveness is a process. This is an awareness, an assessment of how things are, and looking toward what could be.

How much richer our systems could be if we were more accepting of others who we have labeled "different." The process of keeping others out also serves as denial toward wholeness and equality. We understand many systems philosophically, politically, culturally, socially, racially, and theologically.

Whenever rules, laws, or policies are set up to systematically deny others, then we as society are incomplete. We are not whole. There is only one letter difference between **policy** and **police**. If you set up a policy, then it has to be policed. How much of our psyche time and energy is designed to do just that?

Simon & Simon (1990, p. 20) elaborate on the difficult task of completing a journey of forgiveness when they offer, "That is what forgiveness is all about—working through the unfinished business, letting go of the pain and moving on for your sake. You forgive so that you can finally get rid of the excess emotional baggage that has been weighing you down and holding you back; so you can be free, do and be whatever you decide, instead of stumbling along according to the script painful past experiences wrote for you." Forgiveness is so needed in our lifetime so humanity can move toward more life-giving journeys.

Internal growth happens when we look at our lives from singular or multiple aspects:

- emotionally
- physically
- psychologically
- sexually
- spiritually.

External growth happens when we look at our lives from singular or multiple aspects:

- examine our choices
- assess who we are
- critique where we want to be
- examine the course(s) of action we have taken.

Forgiveness as "passage" is not an easily obtainable happening. Burns (*Forgiveness*, 1992, p. 9) forces us to realize that "forgiveness can be a long journey." Each and every day we get up, we take ourselves with us wherever we go and try to make sense out of daily living. Burns (*Forgiveness*, 1992, p. 11) emphasizes that "our feelings are the least dependable part of us. They run deeper than reason; and fluctuate erratically. We may think we should not feel hurt or that we should feel hurt. Either way, we are hurt, and we need to forgive. Whether or not they deserve to be forgiven...WE deserve it."

Our personal and professional worlds provide us with numerous examples of unhealthy events when forgiveness does not occur. To not forgive quite simply means to:

- hang on
- retain hold of
- savor what happened
- dwell on the past
- forcefully plug in to
- place stock in someone/something
- give your power over
- not live in the present
- be focused elsewhere
- live in another moment
- decrease your current power
- take on negativity
- add others of your own...

When we do not forgive, our body lets us know. Our body tracks all of our internal thoughts and mechanisms and "banks" them. Only in recent decades have we begun to make the broad connection of how critically important our body is in serving as an "alarm system." This internal and external alarm system lives out the reality of all our actions. We store all thoughts, content, mannerisms, and reflections inside. Our immune system is continually eavesdropping on our thoughts. We get sick, have headaches, are not relaxed, do not get work accomplished, experience frustration, are moody, do not care, limit our productivity, develop addictions, and in general don't produce at our maximum potential. McDonald (1992, p. 10) emphasizes our "emotional paralysis can effect the adult learner in ways not clearly identified or accepted."

The bottom line in focusing on our lack of forgiveness is quite simply that we hinder life within. We energetically place our psyche elsewhere, sometimes even beyond reach.

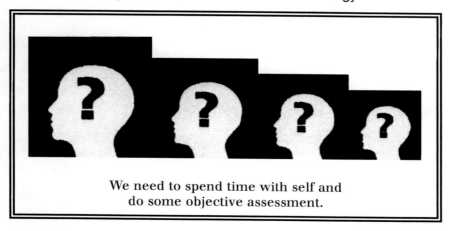

We need to spend time with self and
do some objective assessment.

Looking back on our early years permits most of us to identify some lessons on forgiveness from our childhood. Whether these be formal or informal lessons from family, school, church, or society, there was some input taught to us on this act of forgiveness. In the next section, we will explore a conversation which offers a valuable lesson.

Workshops I've presented in various parts of our country and abroad continually serve as a vehicle for sharing private narratives. Workshop participants disclose personal and, I might add, sacred stories from their past.

Each has a tale or situation someone wanted to share. Many come up during breaks and relate their account. People want to share their stories. They want others to know and experience the awesome freedom that comes from letting go of the past. The forceful act of forgiving is overwhelmingly powerful. Many will say, "Even though I know nothing is changed, I had the need to say I forgive you."

Throughout this text are narratives people chose to share. The settings are varied and are presented in no specified order. They are detailed to give credence to the power of forgiveness in a variety of life experiences.

A PARENTAL MESSAGE

This story left me in awe of the importance of proper and loving parenting. I have rejoiced in it on numerous occasions. Each time I witness parents teaching their children, I come to realize the great gift parents have in raising a healthy and wholesome human being of their very own creation.

At a luncheon, my friend Ro told me this story. She and her husband, Jack, are the parents of three children, ages 11, 13, and 15. Ro related that she taught her children to be aware when they committed an unkind act toward one another or had been the victim of an inappropriate action by another. As young children they were taught to say "I am sorry" or "I forgive you" to the others' statement or action. To this day, this practice is current in their family. The words "I'm sorry" or "I forgive you" are uttered spontaneously! These children were gifted with teaching by parents who knew early on that forgiveness returns energy. The children do not dwell on negativity, nor do they harbor ill feelings towards their siblings or friends. This lesson teaches us that through forgiveness we can take our present energetic abilities and keep them in motion for greater good. We view this graphic and see positive energy in motion.

Energy begets energy!

An act of forgiveness allows energy to be placed here in present time. It mobilizes our forces to be used in the act of creativity rather than dwell on something or someone from the past. An act of forgiveness allows us to localize our energetic forces on current tasks or future accomplishments. When we forgive we can be in the present. We are here *now*! We live for what is and for that which can *be*!

Another way of examining the understanding of forgiveness is to take it all apart, to really investigate its core components. Each of us has to personally examine where we are in the process of understanding, digesting, and acting on the meaning of forgiveness as it relates in a personal way. As we review an examination of this *forgiveness* definition as *"generating internal vital energy,"* we take it in in a very personal way and have a good talk with ourselves.

BIBLICAL REFLECTION

In reflecting on Philippians 1: 3-6; 3:12-16 we read these sacred words.

> I thank my God whenever I think of you; and
> every time I pray for all of you, I pray with joy,

remembering how you have helped to spread
the Good News from the day you first heard it
right up to this present. I am quite certain
that the One who began this good work in you
will see that it is finished when the Day of
Christ Jesus comes.

Not that I have become perfect yet; I have not yet
won, but I am still running, trying to capture the
prize for which Christ Jesus captured me.
I can assure you I am far from thinking that
I have already won. All I can say is that
I forget the part and I strain ahead for what
is still to come; I am racing for the finish,
for the prize in Christ Jesus. We who are called
"perfect" must all think in this way. If there is
some point on which you see things differently,
God will make it clear to you; meanwhile,
let us go forward on the he road
that has brought us to where we are.

In honoring these words, we realize our own imperfections. We ask for guidance and understanding to help us on our journey. Emphasis is placed on realizing we cannot do it alone. Rather we call upon our God to provide us with the aid and understanding to continue the journey. It is in the reflection of the passage above that we can gain new insight into the meaning of forgiveness. Let us dissect and review the meaning of these all important words and action we talk of so freely.

FOR G I V E N ESS Generates Internal Vital Energy

FOR

We have a general understanding of the word 'for,' i.e., to move in the direction, be in favor of, a general feeling of okay. To be for means to be with.

(The opposite would be against!)

<u>G</u>ENERATING

When we evaluate a word like generating, we know it means to produce, to bring something into being; to cause change to occur; to get things going; to bring about what was previously absent or dormant.

(Its opposite would be non-movement!)

INTERNAL
Internal indicates interior, or intimate. We know that internal is contained "behind closed doors." It is not easily identified as its nature is kept secret. The manifestation of internal is known by only a limited source. Its presence is within.

(Its opposite would be external!)

VITAL
We know this means critical. This is indispensable and of crucial importance. For anything to be identified as vital we know that it has energetic force or power. Its presence is life in all matters, shapes, and form.

(Its opposite would be non-existent!)

ENERGY
We know that energy motivates and causes something to happen. The "force" causes change to happen. It is the driving component behind movement. Without energy, life ceases.

(Its opposite would be non-life!)

The comparison of Scripture and the interpretation of the word "forgiveness" presented here enables us to do some reflection and application. If as Scripture states, "I forget the past and I strain ahead for what is still to come," then I must take stock of my life and the choices I have made and continue to make this day. We assess the relationship of life and choices.

In the universal prayer, "The Lord's Prayer," we say, "Forgive us our trespasses, as we forgive those who trespass against us."

FORGIVENESS: IT'S POWER
An act of forgiveness is such a powerful event that when it happens new life begins immediately . Often we are not aware that new life is taking place, but it does. New life-giving energy evolves. An act of forgiveness can cause:

- oceans to part
- relationships to heal
- mountains to move
- systems to unite
- the sky to be lifted
- hearts to light up
- the earth to regenerate
- the human condition to recreate

As Robert Dewey stated, "Education is not just a preparation for life. Education is life." To paraphrase this quote we can also say, **forgiveness is not just a preparation for living life, forgiveness generates life**. Forgiveness is one of those special gifts that can be self-administered. We receive the greatest return on our investment when we do just that. We focus on our choices, make a decision to forgive, then generate internal vital energy so that it can be placed in alternative settings of our lives. A return on that investment provides multiple dividends.

So often we hear of wanting more time, effort, energy and abilities. Well, the answer is right within. Go for it. "Gift yourself!"

When someone experiences the gift of giving through forgiveness, it is amazing how life changes. We realize a sense of renewal. We experience a feeling of new life and energy. We can go about and move into, through, and about places where, previously, we were uncertain, or rather, where we didn't want to go. When we forgive, we recycle ourselves and our world.

Chapter VI

FORGIVENESS: A GLOBAL "I.V."

Forgiveness goes way beyond one human being. What affects a part affects the whole. Let us compare the internal vital aspect of forgiveness with medical understanding. We relate to the medical meaning of an I.V. and its critical importance in sustaining life. We don't even argue with it. Rather we expect it to happen in a hospital or emergency setting. When an I.V. is administered, we back off and allow those in the know to act. We know what is good for the other person.

Authority is given over to the medical personnel to do all within their power to sustain the life of the person in their care. As long as an individual is under medical care, we stand back and believe they will survive. We know the medical (I.V.) is only temporary until the individual can function on his or her own. But as long as medical attention is needed, we acquiesce.

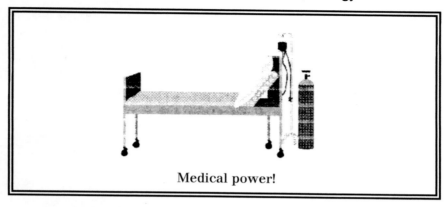

Medical power!

This acknowledgment and placement of medical power is critical in the process of physical healing. We need also look at how we can play an equally important part in the forgiving process as it relates to personal healing. We need to know that what we do does matter. It goes way beyond self and environment.

When we do not let go, we cannot let God be here. Myss in *Anatomy of the Spirit* (1996 p. 40) states, "Our bodies contain our histories—every chapter, line, and verse of every event and relationship in our lives. As our lives unfold, our biological health becomes a living, breathing biographical statement that conveys our strengths, weaknesses, hopes, and fears."

Thus if we look at forgiveness as generating internal vital energy we know and realize the significance of its awesome presence in our lives. We absolutely have no other choice but to live in the present, to forgive, so that the seeds of internal vital energy can grow. Thus we become aware of our personal responsibility for our own on-going creation. We do create our own reality by where we place our energy.

We recognize forgiveness in a much broader scope and realize the connectedness of all things, in all places, all of the time. Myss and Shealy (1987, p. 56) so aptly state, "We are unaccustomed to thinking about planet Earth as having consciousness. Most of us have never considered that the earth exists as a form of life that is independent of the human experience and that, as a form of life, the earth has spirit and intelligence. This is a perception that is not novel to certain spiritual traditions, but many individuals have never given such mystical perceptions scientific or medical credibility, much less serious environmental concern."

The power of global awareness is hitting us full force. The need for global internal vital power is always present. Refusal to forgive can have negative impact on the planet. McDonald (1992, p.11) emphasizes that "we handle our own personal anger by taking inventory of how we respond in all phases of life. We rid ourselves of unpleasantness from our past. We take stock of what we can change. We look at our own behavior and the choices we have developed over time. We need to do a personal inventory and ask ourselves what is worth:

- changing? . . . . .forgetting?
- altering? . . . . .eliminating?
- accepting? . . . . .letting go?
- modifying? . . . . .terminating?

The global impact of forgiveness possesses awesome power and unleashed potential. We can make this happen first by individual effort then escalate beyond ourselves toward a global presence."

Now we move into a study of our past, present, and future visioning of life. Once again we give serious thought to the integration of what has been, is now, and has the potential to become.

Chapter VII

PAST, PRESENT, FUTURE

Visuals give us a concrete way of scrutinizing a situation. Let us view forgiveness with attention to this design.

PAST

PRESENT

FUTURE

Look at the words and symbols. Now focus on where we place our thinking patterns. Where is the locus of our control? In what time frame (past, present or future) do we expend our vital energy? Where we place our thinking process is precisely where our energy goes. It is that arena of our being which gets the attention.

The design of the model allows us to get inner focus. It gives us the ability to get a grip, to gain awareness of the vital life force that is within us.

PAST

Our past is just that. The past is as it was. It is gone! When we stay in our past emotionally, physically, psychologically, sexually, or spiritually, we cannot live in our present. We lose a focus toward what is happening right now (present) and also to what can become (future). When energy is placed in the past, i.e., that which was, our life-force loses creative ability! The more we live in the past, the harder it is to activate the now. Our physical body is in the now, but when psychic energy is in another time and place, then quite honestly, we cannot be fully human, fully alive. We stagnate! Sometimes we can even be considered among "the walking dead."

When thinking about the past, Burns (1992 p. 96) reminds us to "Limit Your Expectations of Forgiveness."

- You many never get a rosy ending.
- You may never be best friends again.
- You may never kiss and make up.
- You may never like them again.
- You may have to let them go out of your life.

The sooner we recognize the past for what is was, the better our present and future can be. Remember the past is *as* it was! It no longer exists in present form (unless we sustain it).

Of course we can always exercise the option of dwelling on negative past events. But ask yourself, Where is it getting me? By sustaining the past, what am I missing in the present? And how can I mobilize for my future well being?

PRESENT

The PRESENT ▮▮▮ is YOU!

The pre*sent* is the here and now. It is a recognition of what is to be, based on what has been. We are *sent* to be wherever we are.

We can interpret the insight this visual provides by asking:

- What do I bring to the now?
- How do I image?
- How am I wrapped?
- Am I inviting?
- Do I bring excitement with my being?
- When others encounter me, do they feel gifted by my presence?
- How is my wrapping designed?
- Is there care in the presentation of self?

All of these questions matter. They are all important in how I image self beyond self. As I pre*sent* and am *sent* into my daily world, what kind of a gift do I image? No one knows you better than you! So take a look. Do you like what you see? What is your current level of satisfaction or dissatisfaction? Is the gift of your presence worth having?

Ask yourself, "Is there some part of me that could use rearranging? What areas can I improve? In the present or gift of myself, what am I sent to do, to be, to give? How do I "gift" those I come in contact with in my daily interactions?"

FUTURE

You are it! The fu*ture* is not here yet, but we are in the process of creating it. What it will look like, what we will look like depends on what we do with the now. Wheatley and Kellner-Rogers (1996 p. 18)

33

proclaim "our range of creative expression increases as we join with others. New relationships create new capacities." The future that is ours is being conditioned by our current connection to past energy. We possess the power to take into the future whatever we want.

McDonald (1992, p. 11) reminds us, "When we look at the price we pay emotionally, physically, psychologically, sexually, and spiritually for not handling our anger, we must ask, Is it worth it? Why am I hanging on and what good has it done me? Unless we rewrite our script, we tend to duplicate it."

That which we have created is already in process. Our future depends on those insights, awarenesses, materials, possessions we now carry. Let us gain further insight into previous thought patterns by looking at the metaphor of nesting dolls.

These nesting dolls provide us with a visual image of where we have been, are now, and can be in our future. They help us look at ourselves and the placement of energy in a forgiving or an unforgiving way.

Many times I have used nesting dolls to give emphasis to a point in a workshop or presentation. I will state that when we see only one, we see only "one." We see where the individual is at this precise moment or current time frame. We do not have insight into or awareness of all their past experiences which are part of their creation. Thus we make judgments based on limited observation. Such restrictions result in inconclusive awareness. We could form poor or inaccurate assessment based on limited insight.

The nesting dolls metaphorically provide a way for each of us to reflect on where, why, and in whom we place our current energy. In viewing them, an internal awareness can manifest itself. We can gain new insight into old patterns. It is only when we stop and reflect, that we gain awareness. To whom, or to what, have we given our locus of control?

When we look at just one doll, that is what we see. However, inside there lays a sum total of all our years. All our experiences, feelings, actions, emotions, events, people, places, things, all that which was once a part of our past is also a part of our now. In summation our past has built our present toward the future we are creating.

In using the nesting dolls in our understanding of forgiveness, we visualize how we have placed our energetic force(s) in an event, a person, a system, or situation of long ago. When we stay in the past, or at some previous developmental or underdeveloped stage of our life, then we limit our current growth and impede future potential.

FORGIVENESS: RETHINKING MY THINKING
By examining and assessing our thinking patterns we gain insight, awareness, viewpoints, and behavioral understanding of what we have chosen to stay connected to in our past experience(s). Reflection on where we are in our chronological patterns, and where we are in our emotional and behavioral patterns, can afford unique ways of knowing.

This places emphasis on the importance of spending time with self and in private meditation. We need to take stock of who and what we are in the various moments of our existence.

In order to have continual growth, we need to stop, reflect, and take hold of a point in time. We need to learn to let go. We might be at one stage chronologically, yet our actions and attitudes are rooted in another stage emotionally or psychologically.

At this point ask yourself when you "self-administered" your last mental and emotional check-up. When did you last take time to "take time." What needs to happen which permits you to set aside time just for you? How important is the taking of time in your life? You realize that:

If we always do what we've always done,
we always get what we've always got!

Forgiveness on any level generates internal vital energy.

Forgiveness is connected to all facets of life. There occurs a genesis of new form when we give up the need to control. Forgiveness is so powerful that we actually experience an energetic force that generates life. As a result of forgiveness we might experience any or all of the following in relation to our personal, our professional, and, most important, our spiritual lives:

- attitude change
- behavioral experiences
- choices
- desirability
- enthusiasm
- freedom
- generosity
- health
- intelligence
- justice
- knowledge
- love
- money
- newness
- optimism
- power
- quality
- relief
- sensations
- truth
- usefulness
- vitality
- wisdom
- x-out
- yearning
- zest

This list includes all things from "A to Z" because we need to realize that every aspect of living life is connected to some other form or being. There is nothing that exists in isolation. We as a people and all of our actions are all connected.

In recent years, we have been made aware of environmental concerns surrounding our earth. It is now time to apply this same insight and awareness to our whole being. The internal and external are connected. The past is related to the present, and our future will be what we create.

FORGIVENESS: THE GENERATION OF INTERNAL VITAL ENERGY

Think about the definition of forgiveness as generating internal vital energy. What else could we possibly want but to be energetically present in all that we do? The achievement of this goal can bring such power.

Gethsemane

Jesus provided us with a model when He placed priority on the power of prayer. In the gospel of Matthew 26: 36-46 we come to understand the power of prayer and reflection.

> Then Jesus came with them to a small estate called Gethsemane, and he said to his disciples, "Stay here while I go over there to pray." He took Peter and the two sons of Zebedee with him. And sadness came over him, and great distress. Then he said to them, "My soul is sorrowful to the point of death. Wait here and keep awake with me." And going on a little further he fell on his face and prayed. "My Father," he said "if it is possible, let this cup pass me by. Nevertheless, let it be as you, not I, would have it." He came back to the disciples and found them sleeping, and he said to Peter, "So you had not the strength to keep awake with me one hour? You should be awake, and praying not to be put to the test. The spirit is willing, but the flesh is weak." Again, a second time, he went away and prayed: "My Father," he said "if this cup cannot pass by without my drinking it, your will be done!" And he came again back and found them sleeping, their eyes were so heavy. Leaving them there, he went away again and prayed for the third time, repeating the same words. Then he came back to the disciples and said to them, "You can sleep on now and take

your rest. Now the hour has come when the Son of
Man is to be betrayed into the hands of sinners. Get
up! Let us go! My betrayer is already close at hand."

In reading this account and thinking about forgiveness, how
often do we meditate on the implication of this story in our lives? We
come to depend, as Jesus did, on the assistance of others. We want
to know we can count on our friends. The Gethesamane story helps
us gain a perspective on the important of taking personal stock in
what we do.

Significant others in our lives are of critical importance to our
growth. They serve, assist, help, and empower us in numerous
ways.

But there are times when we will be by ourselves. We will experience aloneness. How then does forgiveness continue to be an
active part of our existence?

Chapter VIII

PERSONAL/PROFESSIONAL FORGIVENESS

PERSONAL FORGIVENESS

Personal forgiveness is probably the most important aspect in the generation of internal vital energy. Forgiveness first starts with "self." If it doesn't, there is little change for the bigger things of life.

Ask yourself the questions below. Put some thought into your responses as you think about situations you've been in. Then think of your responses in terms of how they have enhanced or inhibited your growth.

<u>PERSONAL</u>

I need help!
What's wrong?
Where am I stuck?
Where is my energy?
What am I hanging onto?
What impedes my growth?
Whom do I need to forgive?
What has colored my viewing?
What can I let go of in my past?
Am I still living out my childhood?
What have I learned about my past which can help my future?

All human beings experience aspects of their lives that are perplexing, difficult, hurtful, traumatic, and challenging. The business of living is a lesson in itself. Life is to be lived fully human and fully alive! Each one of us has experienced many unique situations that force us to take stock of who and what we are. We need to question the placement of our energies. Where do we place our energetic forces? What has happened, past or present, that strips our vitality from us?

Marge Naber (1983 p.7) offers some thought-provoking lines to illustrate the importance of this message.

> "I become whole
> in totally accepting the pieces of life.
>
> I go on to become more me
> in spite of losses that seem devastating-
> yet through them I discovered new strengths
> I otherwise would have never known."

PROFESSIONAL FORGIVENESS
Professional forgiveness takes on such tremendous force that often we are unaware of how it has impacted us. Most of our adult life is spent with others, on a regular basis, sorting out the responsibilities of daily events. We gain our livelihood by performing acts of responsibility which impact others.

So many of our waking moments are spent in environments where we earn our living and interact with others at regular, clockwork intervals. We need to assess where and to whom we give energetic placement in these settings. Our professional arena where we spend at least a third of our adult life offers many choices to look at while assessing the quality of our lives.

One can ask, "Do I need to do some forgiving at work? Am I unforgiving in my interactions with others, thereby limiting mutual growth? Do my vitality and energy get displaced because I am unforgiving? Do I only think of *my* needs?"

Ask yourself the following questions. Then think of your responses in terms of how they have enhanced or inhibited your growth.

PROFESSIONAL

Why am I here?
Am I controlling?
What do I do well?
How much can I, do I, give in?
What can I do about my current position?
How can I improve my present surroundings?
Am I giving the best I have to offer each day at work?
What skills, tools, training, do I need to enhance my image?
How do I benefit by and from my colleagues on a daily basis?
How do I maximize the potential of the other individuals?

If you have answers to those questions, what are you going to do about them? We spend so much of our lives at work with others to achieve some common goal(s). What is it that I take to work each and every day? How do I really better my work situation?

Marge Naber (1983, p. 13) again offers insight to ponder as we go about our day-to-day activities in our professional arena. She states:

"Anticipate tomorrow
as a chance to put into practice
the learnings of yesterday and today.

We are so busy planning for future satisfaction
we miss the creative present."

We really do miss many creative moments at work when we hold onto negative situations, words, events, or happenings. When we do not let others grow beyond an image we lock into our mind, then we lose a great deal of potential in what we can learn from them.

Once again we need to realize the importance of spending so much of our lives at work with others to achieve some common goal(s). What is it that I take to work each and every day? What do I need to let go of, bury, and not let interfere with my daily work

---

chores? What do I do to contribute to the betterment of the work situation?

FORGIVENESS: STOP — LOOK — LISTEN

A simple stop sign can be a great teacher. By stopping, looking and listening we can learn so much. It appears we give little thought to how vitally important we are to each and every day. To each person we encounter, our every word, thought, deed, or action are connected.

I am amazed at these important words, **STOP, LOOK, LISTEN,** that we teach children. We encourage them to think about these words, and perform corresponding actions, so they will be safe and do what is right. How much better off adults could be if we, too, would

STOP — LOOK — LISTEN!

Everyday that we leave our home we have daily reminders to STOP, LOOK, LISTEN. We do this with our mechanical vehicles. We need to do this with our emotional, physical, psychological, sexual, and spiritual vehicles.

Chapter IX

FORGIVENESS: DAILY LIVING

Each of us encounters numerous occasions in our daily lives that teach us about life. We are encouraged to learn the lessons of stories, situations, and happenings that occur regularly. Others can show us the importance of forgiveness in the simplest of ways and often when we least expect it to happen.

A FUNERAL GIFT

While attending a family funeral, I had the pleasure of meeting a person who was also there to say her last good-bye to my cousin, Cliff. She looked at the body of my cousin in the casket and then talked to me about how much Cliff had helped her. While attending services at the Riverside Baptist Church, he was always there to listen, give hope, and let her know she was loved by God. He helped her see that she was loved unconditionally. He provided emotional comfort during their conversations. She related that her faith has been strengthened each time they met by his quiet and assuring presence of God's love for her.

As we talked, Bonnie stated that she had been raised in a religion that no longer energized her as an adult. The teachings of this religion offered her little by way of forgiveness. There was too much placement on policies, procedures, rules, regulations, and ritual. Even the mandate that God only speaks through ordained men serves as a way to deny full participation to half the human population. How sad! She experienced little of the love of God through the dictates of this particular organized religion. Bonnie prayed for and wanted continuation of comfort in the practice of this childhood religion. It was not happening.

Bonnie indicated that she met regularly with her brother and discussed general issues of life. One particular time they met at a restaurant, and the topic of conversation centered on Bonnie's inability to find inner peace. She expressed feelings of emptiness in her spiritual quest.

On numerous occasions she and her brother discussed their painful letting go of this former religion. He encouraged her to give her life over to a higher power. Her brother also shared Bonnie's feelings about these teachings and he, too, became disenfranchised. He prayed and found peace with God through another religion. He had at last found peace with his inner being and forgave his past. With new focus in an alternate belief system, he renewed his energetic forces in all facets of his life. He regenerated himself. He once again generated internal vital energy.

At this particular restaurant meeting with her brother, Bonnie resolved that then and there she would follow her newfound beliefs. She would practice her theological understanding of God within a new context. She joined the Riverside Baptist Church in Windsor, Ontario, Canada, over ten years ago and has found untold peace. What makes this story so significant is that Bonnie noticed as she was leaving the restaurant with her brother, that the name of the restaurant, located at a major intersection, was called *Crossroads*.

Yes, her personal crossroads occurred when she chose to forgive herself and her inability to hang onto a religion that limited her spiritual growth. Bonnie generated internal vital energy when she was able to forgive her past and chose to grasp onto a new religion of choice which brought her closer to her God. Her new freedom provides energy.

JUST WHAT IS FORGIVENESS?

Forgiveness is a means to an alternative end. It is a complex process to comprehend. However, once it has been experienced, we untold benefits are realized. Upon completion of an act of forgiveness we see new life, have renewed energy, and realize creative abilities.

To forgive requires action. It is a verb. It means we make a choice to be involved in alternatives. In this sense it requires action, expression, and movement.

By understanding these two functions of the word forgive and forgiveness, we can realize it tremendous power in situations near and far. We can grasp its significance in all aspects of life. FORGIVENESS therefore is:

- letting go of what once was
- looking forward to what can be
- about getting on with the future
- being active, rather than passive
- taking action to bring about change
- bringing our energetic forces into creation
- the active generation of internal vital energy
- being one who is proactive rather than reactive
- the placement of energies into design, not destruction

Chapter X

FORGIVENESS: NOTED AUTHORS

There are many authorities who have given time and energy to the subject of forgiveness. They have provided us with new vision on this critical and life-enhancing subject. Many of these authors approach the concept of forgiveness from numerous angles. The writings of several focus on quality and quantity of living.

How do we do this and how do we not do that? How are our choices tied into our health? How does forgiveness provide for quality of life? Each author provides a unique "twist" on the subject. Therefore by studying forgiveness from several viewpoints we gain new insight. Some will speak to us more than others. It is interesting to note that all authors are rooted in the profound message of Jesus when He issued the greatest commandment of all which is to "love God and love your neighbor." Simple yet profound! Let us again revisit some significant teachings.

In his delightful book *Miracles Do Happen* (1995 p. 15), Norm Shealy states, "All the current interest in alternative medicine is a long-delayed acknowledgment by the public that conventional, allopathic medicine has ignored the most important aspect of healing: the untapped miracle of the individual's personal will, intuition, and heart." Caroline Myss, in *Anatomy of the Spirit* (1996, p. 215), states "Forgiveness is a complex act of consciousness, one that liberates the psyche and soul from the need for personal vengeance and the perception of oneself as a victim." Myss has gifted our world with her wonderful intuitive awareness by helping us realize we are responsible for the outcome of our own destiny. As Myss states, "...our biography becomes our biology."

These insights provide introspection into both the quality and quantity of our lives.

A lack of forgiveness can be very expensive. Where there is no forgiveness there can be no generation of internal vital energy. Some spend countless parts of their years expending negative energy. They fuel their past. They refuse to forgive and are unaware of living in the present. That energy is internal and vital and is needed as source, as fuel, as motivation.

Adults working with both the *young* or those that are *chronologically gifted* have shared with me that the lack of forgiveness inhibits growth. The inhibition of growth can last a lifetime.

Young children have their world in front of them where they are ready to engage in a creative process. The *young* are ready to look at life, make decisions, and get about the business of living.

The *chronologically gifted* have life experience and much to draw upon. They have a wealth of knowledge to help in their decision-making process.

A lack of forgiveness blocks the path or journey of a person whether *young* or *chronologically gifted* or somewhere in between. This occurs both at conscious and unconscious levels.

As we progress through our life journey we analyze where the placements of our energetic forces have taken us. In looking at where we are, we need to analyze our personal course(s) of action. Each individual is responsible for localizing himself or herself into a situation. Trudy Settel (1995 p. 38) states "When we see that we have gone wrong, it is our duty to retrain our footsteps and proceed."

As soon as we "see," we are then responsible for taking action. When we gain vision we also gain responsibility.

Zalman Schachter-Shalomi and Ronald S. Miller (1995 p. 98) tell us that an inability to forgive can be extremely costly. They state,

> For example, when I refuse to forgive someone who has wronged me, I mobilize my own inner criminal justice system to punish the offender. As judge and jury, I sentence the person to a long prison term without parole and incarcerate them in a prison that I construct from the bricks and mortar of a hardened heart. Now as jailer and warden, I must spend as much time in prison as the prisoner I am guarding. All the energy that I put into maintaining the prison system comes out of my "energy budget." From this point of view, bearing a grudge is very "costly," because long-held feelings of anger, resentment,

and fear drain my energy and imprison my vitality and creativity.

Wow! What a message. We do have to take individual responsibility for creating our own reality. No one can do it for us.

At this point let's do some introspection. What do you see in regard to yourself and your energy?

Ask yourself these questions:

- Why can't I let go?
- Why won't I let go?
- What am I sexually tied to?
- To what am I emotionally tied?
- What do I fear by not forgiving?
- What am I psychologically tied to?
- What keeps me physically restrained?
- Am I hanging onto to something from my past?
- Do I give my power over because I will not let go?
- Can I even remember what person, event, or situation upset me?

The **power** to choose life is always within the person. That, in a sense, is why forgiveness is so powerful. It lies within! Thus, you have the inspiring ability to re-create you. The choice you make in generating life determines birth, growth, milestones, or just merely blurs on your horizon. We can stretch this focus a bit farther by investing in our own thought process. This visualization helps us see that we have to keep in motion. We have to realize and give emphasis to the importance of doing, being, and living.

It is imperative that we stay in motion!

Wheatley and Kellner-Rogers in their book *A Simpler Way* (1996, p. 44), remind us, "Agility and the freedom to be creative are more likely when we focus on what works rather than what's right."

Each person has the gift of creativity. The recognition of another person's creativity can provide new growth from old materials. So often a lack of forgiveness happens because of our sight, our vision of what is truth. A helpful way of analyzing truth can be achieved through the following passage from Mortimer Adler (1981):

> The pursuit of truth in all branches of organized knowledge involves (1) the addition of new truths to the body of settled or established truths already achieved, (2) the replacement of less accurate or less comprehensive formulations by better ones, (3) the discovery of errors or inadequacies together with the rectification of judgments found erroneous or otherwise at fault, and (4) the discarding of generalizations—or hypotheses and theories—that have been falsified by negative instances. (p. 56, 57).

What we internalize as "truth" can often be:

- ignorance
- stubbornness
- a closed mind
- a closed heart
- misjudgment
- incorrect facts
- incomplete pieces
- distortions of reality
- misguided information
- biased opinions/statements
- a lack of thorough understanding

This visual helps us gain insight about how distorted our thinking can be at times.

This images a lack of control, direction, or focus!

Each individual needs to re-evaluate his or her own concept of truth. Often it is precisely within our "truth-vision" that we localize our energy. The quality of life is in direct proportion to our ability to forgive or not to forgive. We are encouraged to look within so that we may forgive without. Caroline Myss and Norman Shealy (1993 p. 28) suggest "there is so little encouragement in our society to foster skills of introspection and self-examination, people do not know how to begin to 'go to work on themselves'."

The computer world we live in provides concrete actuality about future potential. Adults could learn a lot from children. In *The Road Ahead* (1995, p. 191), Gates reflects on untapped capabilities. "Kids and computers get along just great, partly because kids aren't invested in established ways of doing things. Children like to provoke a reaction, and computers are reactive." Kids demonstrate a delightful way of continual learning. We need some self-assessment in all aspects of life. Are we as adults continually learning?

As we gain awareness of our world, we realize we can make changes. Even in our thinking, we can **"rethink."** Bill Gates (1995, p. 255) reminds us, "Most programs have "undo" commands that make it simple to try something, then quickly reverse it." As adults we, too, have an **"undo"** button. It's called forgiveness. How often do we stay stuck in our thinking process? How often do we repeat the same actions?

As adults we have to mandate action and forcibly look **within** so that we may understand the course of our action. Thus we have a better understanding of what is occurring in our world. We can look without with greater clarity. Forgiveness indeed does generate internal vital energy. The act of forgiveness is life-giving. Through the act of forgiveness one comes to realize that it is an act of taking back personal power in all we do. We are encouraged to aim for the center. This visual helps us see the importance of centering. We go for the bullseye!

We must get on target in living life!

We read books, study truths, watch people, pray, ask for inner guidance, and believe that we can bring about change. All these changes can happen but often do not because we limit our own growth by not forgiving. We do this on all levels of our personal and professional lives.

Chapter XI

LIFE SITUATIONS

SIBLING RIVALRY

The multiple situations in daily living provide us with adequate understanding of life experiences. We need only think about the numerous experiences any adult has.

The lack of forgiveness has its own twists and turns. We hold out for hope in understanding the lack of forgiveness. A lack of forgiveness must end, because there is no resurrection without it.

Take the case of an older sister who cannot seem to forgive her younger sister because her younger sister wished to celebrate an anniversary of hers *her* way. In this case, the older sister was not the dominant decision maker. Subsequent to this occasion, the two sisters were very close.

It makes it difficult at family gatherings to say the least. And in spite of several attempts by the younger sister to initiate a reconciliation, to heal this devisiveness, it has not happened.

What is the answer? Prayer is the best answer—always.

Someday, it is hoped, it will end. There can be no peace, growth, or resurrection without forgiveness.

And, again, what about health issues? What happens within a person's body when an individual harbors these negative emotions? One can only guess. Negative emotions have to land somewhere, and often it is right within our own bodies.

In situations like this the best remedy, I believe, is to offer the person to God. Ask God to speak to the person who is withholding forgiveness, to melt her heart, to take away all sadness. We, on our part, must be ready to accept whatever is offered to us by them!

Some people cannot say "I am sorry," but they attempt to show they are in other ways. We must go forth to meet them and use the example of the Prodigal Son. We must "hasten" to meet the other and all will be well, and all will be well. Thus, we will be spiritually free. When we generate life, we get our spirit back.

A LOST SON

In a recent conversation about this book, the topic of forgiveness surfaced. Martie, a professional colleague, shared her story. She related the following insight and awareness concerning a tragic event she experienced in December 1988.

"Ten years ago my son was killed by a drunk driver. It was the hardest thing my family had to go through. My family was deeply grieving for our great loss. But you know, Pat, I had to forgive the young man who took the life of my son. I was not able to speak directly to the young man in court. I did however, speak to his father and told him to tell his son 'I forgive you'."

"Our family was victimized by the loss of my son. Nothing could bring him back. But I know I had to let this other young person know that however painful our loss was (and still is) I forgave him his actions. As a result of that act of forgiveness I derived numerous advantages toward living. I was able to place my energies in a positive direction. The whole experience gives one credentials you get in no other way. Not only the forgiveness, but the tragedy itself."

In a follow-up conversation about this event my colleague stated, "You know, Pat, there is tremendous freedom that comes with forgiveness." As a result of the action she took, her work has been advanced, and moved in a positive direction of life-giving magnitude.

"POWER" ABUSE

Another aspect of forgiveness deals with those in power positions. We are well aware of the abuse of power. Headlines scream this fact at us daily. We are saddened when we hear this and it causes us to ponder more often than not.

Abuse by one in a power position happens more frequently than one would care to admit. Its lasting effects challenges one who attempts to go down the avenue of forgiveness, to truly try to be, and to live as a Christian.

Any employer who attempts to diminish an employee by whatever means she/he chooses to bring about her or his termination is guilty of the abuse of power. Granted there will be personality clashes, conflicts of ideas, and the like, but if one is terminated through lies, deceit, or trumped-up charges, it is not easily swallowed. It will most likely be remembered forever because of the impact on the receiver.

If and when a person comes to terms with her or himself and attempts to forgive the person the terrible injustice, there is quite a heavy load of emotional baggage to lift from one's heart and rinse out of one's system.

Perhaps one can begin with telling God we forgive the person. Maybe later we can talk to the individual. Maybe not! It can be approached in different ways. Praying for the person who wounded us is a good place to start. Meditation on the Our Father is certainly favored. Forgive us our trespasses, as we forgive those who trespass against us! What a loaded statement! We want forgiveness from our God. Do we also grant forgiveness to those who plea to us? It's an interesting thought. Do we give to others, as we request God to give to us? We want a divine power in our life, thus we need to grant that same gift to others.

A DYING MOTHER

In conversing with a college friend, I shared the content and the focus of this book. My friend looked at me and said, "I can identify with the concept, Pat." Our conversation then took the direction of Mimi sharing her last sacred moments with her mother. Her words were awesome.

As her mother lay dying a year ago, Mimi intuited that there was some unfinished business her mother needed to respond to before she left this world. Mimi knew her mother's death was only a short time away, but her mother was just not "letting go" of her spirit. The special bond and trust between a mother and daughter gives credence to the following story Mimi sent to me.

"When my mother lay dying, her heartbeat too faint and irregular to be monitored, her other organs already shut down, yet still, beyond all expectation or possibility, clinging to life, I realized that it was not her 'fighting Irish' spirit I was seeing but rather evidence of a task unfinished, a peace not yet won. It became my task, therefore, to help her to let go, free to move on.

"We (family and friends) had already said our goodbyes, given her permission to die, but she wasn't letting go. Not knowing why, I consulted a friend, a hospice social worker: What had I forgotten? What more could I do? What might her unfinished business be? My friend asked if we had talked about forgiveness, about coming to terms with the past. I said no; but her question hit home, suggesting an extremely sensitive issue I had not thought to explore.

"Less than a year earlier, following my uncle's funeral, I had learned that my grandfather had sexually abused one of my cousins. While devastating to consider—and even more shattering to connect with my mother—it seemed not outside the realm of possibility that a man who would abuse his granddaughter might first have abused his own daughter. But how was I to verbalize this to/for my **mother,** a woman who never spoke about the unspeakable, who put the kindest interpretation on any misbehavior, who made excuses for everyone, whom I had never heard make an unkind remark about anyone, much less her father?

"Because all I had was a suspicion, however strong, I could speak to her in only the most general of terms, broadly applicable statements, sharing my own reflections on life and the inadequacies of being human: how people, wanting and meaning to do what is right, what is best for themselves and others, often do not succeed; how sometimes the very people who should love us the most, who should protect us, whom we most trust, betray us or hurt us deeply; now we don't have to assume either the responsibility or the guilt for those betrayals and hurts; how it's okay to blame others and to feel great anger, even outrage, over being so wronged; how we have to forgive not only the people who have hurt or betrayed us but also ourselves—for 'allowing' ourselves to be hurt, for not being perfect, for whatever; how we all just do the best we can at any given moment, whatever our age—and to expect more of ourselves is simply not fair.

"There was, I know, much more I said to her; but since the words flowing through me were God's, not mine, I don't remember everything.

"What is indelibly etched in my memory, though, is my mother's response. After having barely moved, lying without opening her eyes or speaking for two days, she suddenly tried to sit up. Her eyes flew open, her mouth moved and she clutched my hand so that the powerful current of her emotions, evoked by my words, flowed into and through me as well. And, subsequently, I felt the laying down of her burden, the final relaxation of her tightly held tension she may well have buried and then carried nearly all of her ninety-two years. Whatever the actual facts or circumstances, I will never know—and it really doesn't matter. What matters is that the bonds—guilt? fear? hatred? shame? pain?—of whatever had been holding her back were broken. She who had seemed so easily to forgive so many for so much had, at the last, forgiven and freed herself, finding the peace she sought.

"To close this, our final conversation, I invented a dialogue to help her on her way, reminding her that my father, her brother and his wife were all waiting for her with open arms. The four of them had been so close, sharing so many wonderful experiences together through the years, that the joy of their reunion was easy to imagine. And then I told her that whenever she felt ready to join them, she should just go. As I finished speaking, her faithful caregiver-cum-friend entered the room. I said, 'Mom, the Irish are here. It's time to party!'

"Less than a minute later, she let go, and she let God welcome her."

It amazes me that when the subject of forgiveness enters a conversation, it triggers thoughts. Another example of an individual sharing her story is as follows.

SELF FORGIVENESS...LETTING GO!

The warm months of Summer bring on occasions at the lake, opportunities to vacate daily routines, moments to share in conversation, and a time to reflect. This final personal story outlines just one of those occasions.

Kathleen, a women in her mid-thirties, and I have known one another for about fifteen years. I attended her wedding, know her husband, and have interacted with her three delightful children. She lost her father to cancer last year. As a result of losing the father she dearly loved, an emerging part of Kathleen's persona took uncharted direction. In conversation I asked if she would willingly share her insights on forgiveness. She graciously relates the following.

"Forgiveness? This word takes on a whole new meaning when a significant event takes place in your live. My name is Kathleen, I am thirty-seven years old. The recent death of my father has changed my life drastically. I have taken control of it. It seems as though I lived and gave of myself to others. I often compromised what I wanted to do in order to make others happy. I needed their approval more than my need to do what made Kathleen happy. Many people do not like the changes they have seen in me. Others who are meeting me for the first time...see a more confident, live-life, kind of person. I believe that a death of a loved one does generate energy internally. Some of it a positive energy, some may be self destructive. I have changed in three areas of my life. I have learned to 'forgive and or give' in order to make me whole. I will list them and then explain each one. They are: spiritually, externally, and internally.

"First. Spiritually: I had to learn to forgive God for what had happened to my dad. I know God did not give my dad cancer. I know he did not make my dad smoke for many, many years. What I do know, is my dad suffered greatly. First, through an operation removing parts of his lung. Secondly, through chemo and radiation treatments (took away any quality of life he had). Thirdly, a grueling time of not eating and waking up each morning crying because he was still alive. He was 6' 5" and weighed 295 lbs. At his death he probably weighed 165. I was mad at God for not taking him sooner. I had to learn to forgive God and try to trust that he knew what he

was doing. I had to come to some sort of closure, thinking it was not within my rights to question God's judgment. Even as I type this paragraph, my faith is shaky. I am still working on this issue.

"Second. Externally: I had to forgive my dad and mom, for their role in controlling my environment. They made decisions for me. It was as though I was not allowed to make mistakes of my own and learn from them. They were very protective parents. They did not want unpleasant things to happen to me. They sheltered me from harm. Thus, sheltering me from living life and embracing life for my own. After my dad died, I acquired this overwhelming desire to LIVE.

"Third. Internally: This is the section where I had to learn to GIVE Vs. FORGIVE. I had to learn to give me permission to LIVE life. I want to experience LIFE. I want to make my own mistakes and learn from them. I want to take responsibility for me and my actions. Thus the internal vital energy was created. I have begun to use this energy to accomplish all the many things I need to do in my life, before it is time for me to leave it behind. One example is, I went out and bought a Harley Davidson. That was something I always wanted and I (and my husband) went out and bought it. I am enjoying LIFE a bit more. I have also been disappointed by things as well. The safety net of my dad is no longer there. It took me 35 + years to become Kathleen. I joke because my youngest daughter is so true to herself. She is so sound, stubborn, and her own person already. What took her two years has taken me 35!

I close with two reflections I have heard recently.

"1). I decided my life would be a total success if I could make just ONE person happy. I PICKED ME! When one first reads this statement it can be taken as a selfish one in nature. I chose to see the good in it. I realize that people can aid in the effort to make me happy, but, only I have the power within myself to make Kathleen happy.

"2). For a long time it had seemed that life was about to begin. There was always some obstacle in the way. Something to be gotten through first, some unfinished business, time to be served, a debt to be paid. Then life would begin. At last it dawned on me that the obstacles were 'MY LIFE.'

"This has made me see there is no special way to happiness. Happiness is the way. Treasure every moment, share those moments with someone, time waits for no one."

The personal reflections provide insight and awareness about our ability to continually create. It is about the generation of internal vital energy making a difference.

Will we remember events, situations, happenings, words, actions? Of course we will. Dietrich Bonhoffer, a theologian, says,

"Forgiveness is forgetting in spite of remembering." It may take years. A great motivation is to be "right" before God. What else is there? Be assured we will be at peace when we forgive.

FORGIVENESS IN SYSTEMS

> Yesterday is history.
> Tomorrow a mystery.
> Today is a gift.
> That's why it is called the present!

Each of us is plugged into many systems. McDonald (1992, p. 43) encourages us to realize that, "As we assess systems we engage in, we must determine whether they are bad-indifferent-good. Each of us determines the placement of our personal energy in the design and maintenance of the systems of which we are a part." The ebb and flow of our lives bring us into contact with many groups. It is imperative that we maintain guard in all systems in which we are engaged. According to McDonald (1992, p. 43), "Our world knowledge web enables us to access alternate views. We have the capability to see beyond our current scope." Let's look at some of the ways we are connected.

All of these various systems have connections to us, and we to them. We can assist, or resist these systems in our lives. If we have had negative effects from any of our past systems, then often we tend to leave our energy there. A backward presence prevents us from living in present time. Rather we plug into our past. We do not forgive. When we plug into the past we all suffer. We limit our connected growth!

Systems:
Family . . . . .of origin, nuclear, extended, spiritual
Professional . . . . . .direct, indirect, extended,
Organizations . . . . .local, national, global
Interests . . . . .personal, professional
Other . . . . .church, local connections, interest groups

Chapter XII

FORGIVENESS: A "NEW" YOU

The biblical imperative that we "forgive seventy times seven" really can have profound effects. That is, if we let it happen.

To create a healthy life, an enriching environment, a purposeful existence, I suggest we look at how we hold ourselves back from realizing our dreams, our goals in life. It is imperative that we look at our own act of forgiveness and how that has a hold on our life. Forgiveness means generating internal vital energy.

FORGIVENESS

Do I generate?
Is it internal?
How vital is it ?
How energetic is it?

These are important questions to ask ourselves.

Through forgiveness we *give* and in the giving we realize what we do for self. By the act of forgiveness we insert an I.V. G*IV*E (an I.V. is an intravenous feeding). Forgiveness generates internal and vital energy. We really give ourselves new life when we commit an act of forgiveness. Myss and Shealy (1987, p. 70) remind us with the insight of one individual. "Before I was ill, I did not have any sense of spirituality. I had religion. I practiced a form with no belief in its substance. As a result of being ill, I was able to connect the substance to the form." We can generate internal vital energy! Now isn't that a delightful gift!

A reflection on forgiveness permits us to delve into pieces of our lives. We look at our life as a mosaic, a weaving, a journey. We look at what has caused growth opportunity or what has served as limitation. Forgiveness is indeed a very personal thing but at the same time a powerful, all energizing awesome opportunity for new growth and development. Take some time, just for you and ponder.

Reflection questions regarding forgiveness.

Question	Reflection
Where can forgiveness take me?	Where do you want to go?
How important is forgiveness?	Look at the quality of your life?
What must I do to achieve it?	What do you want to do?
Is it hard?	It's harder not to forgive?
Can it really make a difference?	Talk to those who have forgiven.
Will my life be different?	Try it and see!
What if I choose not to forgive?	You always have that choice.
What if the she/he won't change?	And so!
I don't want to forgive that person?	You have that option!
I'd never be happy knowing I let them get away with all the things that were done to me.	Are you happy NOW?

Our world has been changed, doors have opened up, new insight has been gained. When we forgive, we give life. We give life primarily to ourselves. Everything else has a residual effect. Once again we reflect on the awareness we have received from computer knowledge exposure. Gates, in *The Road Ahead* (1995, p. 254), believes, "The premium that society pays for skills is going to climb, so my advice is to get a good formal education and then keep on learning. Acquire new interests and skills throughout your life."

Keep your creative energy lit !

Once again we turn to Marge Naber and reflect on her wise words in the living out of our existence. She is optimistic by choice. Her poetry challenges us with these thoughts.

I'm not sure what I can accomplish
in life's endeavors
but I'm filled with the desire to become more
in each step of the process.

FORGIVENESS: PERSONAL INSIGHT AND AWARENESS

Places where forgiveness can begin might include areas of our past and present wherein we are less than satisfied. Simon & Simon (1990, P. 37) remind us that, "The size of your wounds does not matter, however. It is absolutely pointless to compare how you were hurt and how someone else was hurt. Just listen to how ridiculous it sounds to say, 'I shouldn't feel bad about being physically abused because I was never sexually molested,' or, 'I guess I should be glad my parents only hurt me by getting divorced instead of hurting me by being alcoholics.' Whatever happened to somebody else did not hurt you. What happened to you did, and if it hurt, it hurt."

Think about how much energy goes to areas of life and living over which we have no control. Much of life is done, finished and behind us, yet we continually infuse it with negative energy. Simon & Simon (1990, P. 37-38) emphasize "It does matter that you were hurt—regardless of how or when. That painful disappointing experience really happened. You can try to deny its effect on you, avoid thinking about it, or ignore the emotions it provokes. You can try to run away from it, turn it upside down or inside out, or bury it under work, food, sexual activity, or drinking and drug use, but the memories remain in your mind and the emotions well up unexpectedly and often. They are a force to be reckoned with as are the mixed emotions you may feel about the people who hurt you."

Personal insight and awareness afford an opportunity to see where we might begin to change perceptions. The following could be included in locations where we have not forgiven:

- self
- family
- parents
- siblings
- image
- education
- schooling
- home
- work
- background
- people we have worked for/with

This list could go on and on. Myss, in *Why People Don't Heal and How They Can* (1997, p. xix), says in such a powerful way "forgiveness frees up the energy necessary for healing." The point is that when we truly forgive and let go of negative energy, then we experience a surge for life.

When we realize this then we truly know that "forgiveness"

Generates

Internal

Vital

We know we are closer to the promised land. The personal, professional and the divine is living within our reach. Our resurrection has only just begun! A spirited life, a life with spirit, is ours! Forgiveness means forgiving!

Reference List

Adler, Mortimer. J. *Six Great Ideas*. New York: Collier Books, 1981.

Bass, Ellen and Davis, Laura. (1988) *The Courage to Heal*. New York: Harper & Row, 1988.

Burns, Maureen. *Forgiveness*. Greenville: Empey Enterprises, 1992.

Bolton, Robert. *People Skills*. New York: Simon & Schuster, Inc., 1979.

Erikson, Erik H. *The Life Cycle Completed*. New York: W.W. Norton & Co, 1985.

Gates, Bill. *The Road Ahead*. New York: Penguine Books, 1995.

Gilligan, Carol. *In A Different Voice*. Cambridge: Harvard University Press, 1982.

Goleman, Daniel and Gurin, Joel. *Mind/Body Medicine*. New York: Consumer Report Book, 1993.

McDonald, Patricia L. *MAACE Options*, "Handling anger: insights and awareness for the adult learner." Vol. 8, No. 2, p. 10-11, 1992.

McDonald, Patricia L. *Ethics & Critical Thinking Journal*, "THINK: Thoughts Help Intuit New Knowledge," Franklin Publishing Co. Arlington, TX: Issue 408, Vol. 38, p. 58-64, 1997.

McDonald, Patricia L. *Insights for a Changing World*. "SYSTEMS: Sharing Your Soul To Energize Membership," Franklin Publishing Co. Arlington, TX, Vol. 1, p. 43-46, 1997.

Myss, Caroline M, and C. Norman Shealy. *The Creation of Health*. Walpole, NH: Stillpoint Publishing, 1993.

Myss, Caroline M, and C. Norman Shealy. *AIDS: Passageway to Transformation*. Tronto: Fitzhenry & Whiteside Ltd, 1987.

Myss, Caroline M. *Anatomy of the Spirit*. New York: Random House, Inc, 1996.

Myss, Caroline M.. *Intuition.* "Anatomy of the Spirit" Issue 13, October, p. 30-37 & 54-55, 1996.

Myss, Caroline. *Why People Don't Heal and How They Can.* New York: Harmony Books, 1997.

Naber, Margaret. *Alive—In Moments of Becoming Whole.* Utica, MI: Poetry Book, 1983.

Neufeldt, Victoria, editor. *Webster's New World Dictionary.* New York: Warner Books, 1990.

Payne, Thomas. Futurework. Albuquerque: Lodestar, 1996.

Schachter-Shalomi, Zalman and Miller, Ronald S. *From Age-ing to Sage-ing.* Warner Books, 1995.

Settel, Trudy S. *The Book of Gandhi Wisdom.* New York: Carol Publishing Group, 1995.

Shealy, Norman. *Miracles Do Happen.* Rockport: Element Books Inc., 1995.

Simon, Sidney B., and Simon, Suzanne. *Forgiveness.* New York: Warner Books, 1990.

Wheatley, Margaret, Kellner-Rogers, Myron. *A Simpler Way.* San Francisco: Koehler Publishers, Inc, 1996.

Webster's New World Dictionary, Victoria Neufeldt, Editor in Chief. New York: Warner Books, 1990.